WITHDRAWN

POCKET STUDY SKILLS

Series Editor: **Kate Williams**, *Oxford Brookes University, UK*

Illustrations by Sallie Godwin

For the time-pushed student, the *Pocket Study Skills* pack a lot of advice into a little book. Each guide focuses on a single crucial aspect of study giving you step-by-step guidance, handy tips and clear advice on how to approach the important areas which will continually be at the core of your studies.

Published

14 Days to Exam Success

Analyzing a Case Study

Blogs, Wikis, Podcasts and More

Brilliant Writing Tips for Students

Completing Your PhD

Doing Research

Getting Critical (2nd edn)

Planning Your Dissertation

Planning Your Essay (2nd edn)

Planning Your PhD

Posters and Presentations

Reading and Making Notes (2nd edn)

Referencing and Understanding Plagiarism

Reflective Writing

Report Writing

Science Study Skills

Studying with Dyslexia

Success in Groupwork

Time Management

Where's Your Argument?

Writing for University (2nd edn)

Pocket Study Skills

Series Standing Order
ISBN 978-0-230-21605-1
(outside North America only)

You can receive future titles in this series as they are published by placing a standing order. Please contact your bookseller or, in case of difficulty, write to us at the address below with your name and address, the title of the series and the ISBN quoted above.

Customer Services Department, Macmillan Distribution Ltd, Houndmills, Basingstoke, Hampshire, RG21 6XS, UK

POCKET STUDY SKILLS

Vanessa van der Ham

ANALYZING A CASE STUDY

macmillan education palgrave

First published 2016 by
PALGRAVE

Palgrave in the UK is an imprint of Macmillan Publishers Limited, registered in England, company number 785998, of 4 Crinan Street, London, N1 9XW.

Palgrave Macmillan in the US is a division of St Martin's Press LLC, 175 Fifth Avenue, New York, NY 10010.

Palgrave is a global imprint of the above companies and is represented throughout the world.

Palgrave® and Macmillan® are registered trademarks in the United States, the United Kingdom, Europe and other countries.

ISBN: 978-1-137-56620-1   paperback

This book is printed on paper suitable for recycling and made from fully managed and sustained forest sources. Logging, pulping and manufacturing processes are expected to conform to the environmental regulations of the country of origin.

A catalogue record for this book is available from the British Library.

A catalog record for this book is available from the Library of Congress.

Printed in China

Contents

Acknowledgements

Thank you to the students at Massey University who've shared their case study assignments with me over the years. Your questions, concerns and insights helped to generate many of the ideas for this book. Thank you also to my colleagues and friends for their assistance with researching the book and for critical review – particularly Jane Terrell, Jenni Beckett, Lisa Stewart, Fiona Diesch, Lynn Randall and Jay Smith. Thanks also to Massey University for permission to use my Moon Dust case study and notes.

Special thanks to Kate Williams, Helen Caunce and Georgia Walters for their advice and encouragement. Thanks also to Sallie Godwin for her fabulous illustrations that contribute so much to the book, and to Maggie Lythgoe, copyeditor, and the editorial and production teams at Palgrave for making the book happen.

Finally, a huge thank you to Mark for all his support and feedback during the writing process.

Introduction

Case study assignments have become a regular feature in university courses at undergraduate and postgraduate levels of study.

The thinking behind using case study assignments is that you get a deeper understanding of the theories, concepts and strategies being taught on the course if you actually *use* them instead of just reading about them. So, your tutors give you descriptions of real-life situations or 'cases', which fit with the material being taught in the course, and ask you to apply your understanding of this material to analyze the situation in the case.

A case study assignment might ask you to:

- **Provide a solution to a problem:** Speech and Language Therapy students, for example, are asked to design an intervention programme for a client with a particular condition.
- **Provide an explanation for *why* something happened:** Engineering students might be asked to provide a group report explaining why a particular building collapsed during an earthquake.

This book concentrates mainly on cases requiring a solution to a problem but much of the advice can also be applied to cases requiring an explanation for why something happened as well. In both situations, your tutors are looking for an analysis of the **causes** of the problem. Without a clear understanding of causal factors, any solution is likely to fail.

If engineers don't have a clear understanding of **why** buildings fail to stand up to earthquakes, they are likely to make the same mistakes in designing new structures.

Answering the why questions is really what case study analysis is all about:

▸ **Why** is this happening/has this happened?
▸ **Why** would my proposed solution work?

And answering these questions involves providing a **critical analysis** of the situation using what you're learning in your coursework.

Don't be intimidated by the term 'critical analysis' here. You use critical analysis all the time to solve problems in your own life. For example, you go for a few job interviews and don't get the job. So you start asking the why questions and trace back the reasons or causes for your failure to get the job. Was it the clothes I was wearing? My CV? The interviewer's attitudes? And maybe you go online to consult the experts in interviewing techniques (recruitment agencies perhaps) and then compare what you've been doing with what they say you *should* be doing – best practice in interviews. In this way, you're critically analysing the interview situation in the light of what the experts say, drawing your conclusions about what you're doing wrong, then working out solutions to your problem, weighing up these solutions (suit/no suit?) and deciding on a course of action.

And that's pretty much what you'll be doing in case study assignments – except that the expertise you turn to for answers to the why questions will be the theories, concepts and strategies from your coursework.

This book will take you step by step through the process and provide suggestions for dealing with some of the main concerns students have shared with me in answering case study assignments:

▶ How do I identify the most important facts in the case? There's so much information!
▶ What do I do when there's information missing from the case?

- How do I know which theory and concepts to apply to the case? There are so many of them in the textbook!
- The tutor keeps telling us to make sure we're analyzing the case instead of just describing it. What does she mean? How much of the case should I include in the analysis?

The book uses sample case study assignments throughout to illustrate advice provided on these and other concerns.

PART 1

UNDERSTANDING CASE STUDY ASSIGNMENTS

1 What is a case study?

You may have seen cases used as examples in textbooks. The cases are descriptions of real-life situations or events and they're included to help students understand theoretical principles by seeing them *applied* in real-life situations.

You'll find that tutors are using cases more and more in their teaching, not only as examples, but as the basis for classroom activities and assignments. The tutor provides a case that mimics a real situation you might encounter in the workplace and you apply what you've learned in the course to study (analyze) the situation.

So:

- A **case** is a real-life situation or event
- A **case study** is an analysis of that situation or event using course materials.

Some of your tutors may also refer to cases as **scenarios**.

Case examples	Analysis of the case
Fast track to nowhere A description of a situation in which a newly appointed CEO of a freight company is facing resistance from a group of managers to changes she is introducing.	Students write a report for the CEO in which they explain why the managers might be resisting the changes and make recommendations about what could be done about it.
Uniform too far? A video that simulates a conversation between senior prefects and teachers who are debating whether or not a pupil should be required to remove a nose stud that has cultural significance for her.	Students write an essay in which they explain why the situation facing the school constitutes an ethical dilemma and use a theoretical framework to assist the school in making a decision about what to do.
Covering the future A description of a rural village where people rely on unsustainable materials for construction of their roofs.	Working in groups, students design a cost-effective roofing system for homes in the village. They present their solution using slides.

You can see there are three parts to the case study assignments here:

The case
- Description of situation
- Video clip
- Description of village

Analysis using course materials:
- Journal articles
- Books
- Government reports
- Codes of practice
- Standards

Outcome
- Report
- Essay
- Slide presentaton

This book focuses mainly on the first two parts – the case and the analysis of the case. Extracts from case study assignments in various subject areas are used to illustrate tips for analyzing the case. See *Report Writing* (Reid, 2012) and *Planning Your Essay* (Godwin, 2009) in this series for advice on structuring your assignments.

Case studies basically follow a **problem-solving[1]** loop. Depending on your assignment brief, yours may include some or all of these steps:

[1] Problem solving is often discussed in terms of moving from a problem situation to a 'desired situation' (see for example Huber, 1980).

Your tools for the job: coursework materials

In order to do this you're going to be examining the case (people, conversations, facts, figures, events) in the light of what you're learning in your course. You'll be using the coursework as a **critical lens** to provide insights into the problem in the case and what can be done about it.

Marking guides for case study assignments explain it something like this:

> Provides a balanced, critical examination of the facts in the case in light of relevant theory and research to provide well-supported conclusions about underlying causes of issues identified in the case and how these can be addressed.

Follow the clues ... make the connections ... draw your conclusions

The process

This involves first reading the case and gathering together the **key facts** of the case (description), then working out how these key facts **fit together** to result in the problem, and how they can be pieced back together to create a solution (analysis).

Description of the case (context)	What are the key facts/issues? • Who? What? Where? When? How? Why?
Analysis of the case using resources and techniques from coursework	How do these key facts/issues **fit together** to result in the current situation? • What are the underlying problems? • What are the causes of these problems? How can the situation be resolved? • What are the possible solution options? • What are the strengths and limitations of these options? • Which solution(s) fits best? How can the solution be implemented? • What is the recommended plan of action? • How can this action plan be monitored for success?

Case study assignments will differ from course to course in terms of:

▶ which elements of analysis are required

▶ which resources and techniques should be used for the analysis.

3 Reading the assignment brief

Case study assignments usually have some kind of description of the requirements for your analysis. These requirements are often set out by your course tutor but sometimes your tutor might refer you to a brief set up by an outside organization, such as a charity seeking a solution to a problem in a developing country.

The brief will contain crucial information about **what** you have to do in the case study assignment and **how** you need to do it. I'm going to look at a few examples of assignments from different subject areas.

From a Management assignment brief:

> Read the case study entitled *Crossing the Floor at Moon Dust Designs* in your course guide. In this assignment you are required to take on the role of a consultant who has been hired by the owner of the company to write a report recommending how to address the problems being experienced in the company.

Elements of analysis required:

1 Note that the actual nature of the problems isn't identified in this brief so you'll have to **identify the issues** in the company that need to be addressed.

2 Although it doesn't actually say so in the brief, it's expected that you will then **analyze the causes** of these problems so that you can …

3 Provide recommendations on what should be done about them.

Resources from coursework:

This brief does not specify any theoretical models to be used for the analysis or any specific perspective to be taken, so it's entirely up to you to choose which theories and concepts to apply to this case. You will be expected to draw on a **range of key theories and concepts** from your coursework and to support your arguments with **evidence from research**.

From a Pre-School Education assignment brief:

> Read the case entitled *Dylan in Charge* in Chapter 3 of your textbook. Write an essay in which you use ecological systems theory and at least one other theory to analyze the case and provide possible explanations for Dylan's aggressive behaviour in the classroom. Suggest two strategies the teacher can use in the classroom to manage Dylan's behaviour.

Elements of analysis required:

Unlike the previous brief, this one identifies the problem in the case: Dylan's aggression. Your task is to identify the causes of this aggression and suggest strategies the teacher can use based on these causes. Note any specifications in the brief regarding numbers etc.

Resources from coursework:

Sometimes tutors specify a particular theoretical model to be used. The theory identified in the brief will serve as the main framework for your analysis of the case. But no single theory can provide all the answers on a topic, so your assignments will require you to refer to other theories and key concepts from the coursework as well and to support your analysis with evidence from research.

Where can I find information on key concepts, theories and research?

The best place to start is your **reading list** for the module combined with the guidance provided by **lecture and tutorial notes**. Tutors often introduce the most important theories and concepts in class and prescribe readings to be done before the class to help prepare you for the discussion. In first-year and other introductory courses, these readings will often come from the **prescribed textbook** for the course, which is often an introductory textbook.

Source 1: introductory textbooks

Introductory textbooks are designed to do exactly what they claim to do – introduce the reader to the **key concepts** and **theories** in an area of study and show how these are applicable in the real world of work. These texts are written for students who are new to the area of study and often include lots of features that can help the reader to understand the contents, including easy-to-follow examples and cases that bring together and illustrate the concepts and theories studied in chapters.

If you are a postgraduate student entering a new area of study for the first time, these books can be really valuable as an introduction. Ask the department which introductory books are prescribed or have been prescribed recently and see if they're available in the library. Sometimes, tutors will put copies of prescribed texts on short-term loan in the library. You don't have to read the whole book – you can use the **Table of Contents** and **Index** of the book to search for information you need.

Use examples and cases in textbooks and lecture notes to help you understand key concepts and theories.

Source 2: journal articles

Example:

Hong J S and Espelage D L (2012) A review of research on bullying and peer victimization in school: An ecological system analysis. *Aggression and Violent Behaviour*, 17(4): 311–22.

This review article uses the theoretical framework specified in the aggression assignment case, so it will provide students with information on the model and its application to the broader problem in the case. Review articles tend to group findings under headings and subheadings so they provide easy access to information. Articles like this also often provide descriptions and applications of related theories on the topic studied, so they can offer great models for how to do this in your own writing.

Reviews of research are also really good starting points to lead you to **research on the topic** – this article has references to nearly 200 readings, many of them studies.

Your friendly library
SEARCH

Ecological systems theory

| AND | bullying |

| AND | school |

Why will I need to refer to research on the topic?

Research provides **evidence** to support your arguments. Theoretical arguments alone without evidence from research won't convince your readers. They need evidence from studies that something in the case *could* cause the types of issues/problems being experienced in the case and evidence that your solution *could* work and why it could work.

Part 3 will take a closer look at the use of evidence to support your arguments in your analysis of the case and provide extracts from case study assignments showing how theory and evidence are used to form an argument and support it.

4 What if I have to find my own case to analyze?

Your assignment might have specifications as to size, location, sector, industry and so on and you need to find an organization that matches them.

Check the analytical reports and directories that are available in library **subject guides**.

Also check out freely available sites such as the **Financial Times Content Hub**, which covers UK-based companies and selected international companies. The site provides company reports and links to current news articles.

You can also look at stock reports in the business pages of **newspapers** and the general

I usually specify that the organization chosen must be at least one year old and must employ a number of people so that the roles and functions covered in the coursework are represented.

Students should look at organizations with easily accessible information so that they can quickly assess whether or not an analysis will be possible.

Tutor

news sections. Newspapers carry stories about all kinds of organizations – use these to link[1] to potential cases.

Remember that when you're choosing your own organization as a case, you need to include enough contextual information in your assignment presentation to serve as a foundation for your analysis – your audience might not know anything about the organization.

What if I have to choose an issue/problem to analyze in my host organization?

Some assignments require you to identify and investigate an issue/problem in your host organization – the organization in which you're doing your work experience or your internship, or where you work. Choosing a problem to investigate can be really tricky because of constraints such as assignment deadlines, access to information, and the data collection methods specified by the brief.

Two issues to check before deciding on a problem:

---

[1] Remember that news articles are not academic sources – use them for links only, not as sources of fact or analysis of organizations.

- **Can you access data or other information using the methods specified in the brief?** If the problem is sensitive for the organization, they might not want you to chat to staff informally about it or interview or survey anyone. So, if those are the methods required, choose another problem.

- **Does the problem fit the scope of the assignment?** If you're writing a report as one of your assignments for a paper, you're going to have very limited time to do your investigation. Be careful that you're not choosing a doctoral studies sized problem for a single assignment.

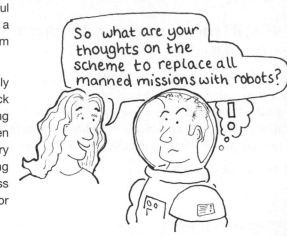

Assignment briefs will usually specify that you need to check with the tutor before deciding on a topic. Once you've chosen and this has been approved, try to avoid panicking and changing topics halfway through unless there's a really good reason for doing so!

5 Reading with a critical mindset

The information in the case provides the *context* for the problem – the setting or circumstances in which the problem is occurring. The *details* of this context are crucial for understanding the problem and how it can be resolved.

Doctors can't begin to diagnose what's wrong with patients until they have all the necessary facts in front of them, which is why doctors ask so many questions!

If crucial information is missing – if the patient lies to the doctor, for example – the diagnosis of the problem is likely to be inaccurate and the solution provided could be ineffective and even harm the patient.

The cases you analyze at university need the same careful scrutiny. They'll have lots of key components that will need to be identified before you can proceed with your analysis. But like the doctor, you are often faced with a whole lot of information you need to sift through and make sense of. This is because your cases are designed to mimic real-life situations, which are multifaceted and often messy.

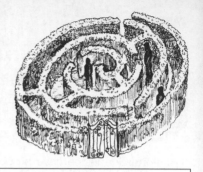

Problem situations at work don't present themselves in a neatly ordered way like a textbook. There are people with different opinions wanting to be heard or nobody's speaking at all. Some crucial information may be missing and some of the information you do have is not relevant to finding a solution for the problem.

So, reading a case is not a passive exercise – you need to pick through the information carefully and decide:

- What are the key facts/issues in the case?
- Which information do I have?
- Which information do I need to find out?

Creating hooks in your mind to catch information in the case

When your brief specifies a particular theoretical model or tool, this provides the starting point for identifying what's important in the case. A clear understanding of the model will create hooks in your mind to catch the important information in the case. Also, remember to look through your lecture notes and do any readings the lecturer has recommended before you start.

Put the case onto the framework (literally!)

You can draw up a graphical representation of the model on a sheet of A3 paper and insert notes from the case as you read. Make sure you include arrows to show relationships so you don't lose sight of these in your reading. This also helps you to *see* the case through the lens of the theory. If your readings provide a graphical representation, use this. If they don't, you can often find quite good representations on Google Images, for example. Just make sure you check them for origin and for accuracy with the model before you use them!

Reading strategically

Read through the case carefully at least twice and note anything that stands out for you. Don't rush this reading – you could miss something important in the case. Like a detective at a crime scene, you'll be carefully sifting through a whole lot of information, deciding which details are important, and starting to group them together. You're establishing the **context** for your analysis here – getting in the vital details.

Six **strategic questions** are often used to get started in a reading or writing task and they'll be a great tool to get started on your case:

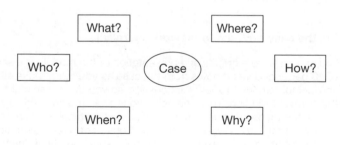

Establishing the context of the case

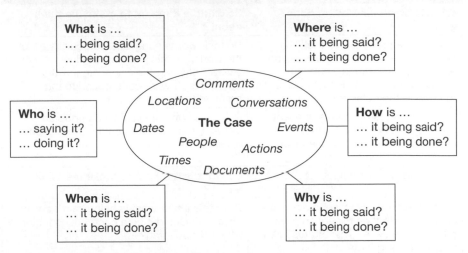

On your second reading, start asking **further strategic questions** about the details of the case:

- Why has this detail been included? Is it key to the case?
- What is it meant to make me think about?

Establish the context	Start making connections to the problems
What is being said/being done?	**So what is it meant to make me think about?**
Is someone presenting a fact? An argument? An opinion? Does anyone else in the case agree with them? Disagree with them? Is there evidence to support their claims?	Do their words suggest a particular view of the world? Is this just an individual view or a view reflecting the whole organization? Could this view be contributing to the problem?
Is there a series of actions or events? Are they related to each other? Are they related to conversations/ statements in the case?	Do the actions or events lead up to an incident in the case? Could they be seen as causal in the event?
Who is saying it/doing it?	**So what is it meant to make me think about?**
Is the person a key stakeholder in the case? What is their relationship with others in the case? Their status? How trustworthy are they?	Does this affect what is being said/done in the case? Could it be a contributing factor to what is happening?

When is it being said/being done?	So what is it meant to make me think about?
Is there a chronological (time) sequence linking conversations/ actions/events? Is there a sense of *before* and *after*? Have things changed over a period of time?	Could they have had a cumulative effect – resulting in the situation? Could they point to an underlying problem? Does the literature suggest that changes like these can cause problems?
Where is it being said/being done?	**So what is it meant to make me think about?**
In a hospital ward? A rest home? In a particular country/city/organization? What kind of organization? How big is the organization – how many people does it employ? How many does it service?	What are the constraints imposed by this environment on the person speaking or acting? Is this action/behaviour understandable or appropriate in this setting?
How is it being said/being done?	**So what is it meant to make me think about?**
Is there a particular tone being used? Vocabulary indicating anger? Threat? Intimacy? Impatience? Is correct procedure being used? Is there evidence in the case of any incorrect procedure at any stage?	Is this something that seems characteristic of the organization as a whole or just a single person? Is there evidence in the readings that this tone/attitude behind the tone can contribute to the kinds of problems being experienced in the case?

Why is it being said/being done?	So what is it meant to make me think about?
In response to something said or done? Something that should have been done? In response to organizational requirements?	Is there some kind of gap in organizational policy or procedures that is leading to the situation? Is there a lack of leadership on an issue?

Sample case exercise: What are the key facts/issues?

We're going to look at the case from the Moon Dust Designs assignment. Read through the case and decide which of the elements provided in the case will be key to our analysis and which could be crossed off as being irrelevant. Also see if you can decide: *What are the priority issues – the most urgent issues that the owner of the company needs to address?*

Compare your answer with mine on the next page. I've used bold print to indicate issues that should be prioritized.

Crossing the Floor at Moon Dust Designs

A passionate clothing designer since the age of 15, Sandra started Moon Dust Designs with the aim of designing and producing quality children's clothing. For the first few years she ran the company from home with the help of three machinists but demand for her clothing increased quickly and last year she hired a cutter, seven more machinists and a supervisor and took out a five-year lease on a factory premises. But with the increase in staff numbers, problems have begun to emerge, with tension between the machinists and supervisor and costly mistakes: 'The machinists are wasting expensive materials and getting more and more careless in their work', Sandra explains, 'and this is leading to delays in production. Everybody's shouting at everybody and last month one of my clients threatened to cancel next season's order because of delays in delivery.' Sandra admits that while she interacts regularly with the cutter and the supervisor, she avoids contact with the machinists because she doesn't feel welcome on the factory floor: 'I just can't believe how much things have changed! We used to chat about work all the time and where we were going with the company. Now I don't even want to walk through their area. They seem to hate me.' One of her most competent and experienced machinists resigned last month and Sandra's worried that others may follow. She's hired you to help her sort out the problems.

Crossing the Floor at Moon Dust Designs

A passionate clothing designer since the age of 15, Sandra started Moon Dust Designs with the aim of designing and producing quality children's clothing. For the first few years she ran the company from home with the help of three machinists but demand for her clothing increased quickly and last year she hired a cutter, seven more machinists and a supervisor and took out a five-year lease on a factory premises. But with the increase in staff numbers, problems have begun to emerge, with tension between the machinists and supervisor and costly mistakes: **'The machinists are wasting expensive materials and getting more and more careless in their work'**, Sandra explains, **'and this is leading to delays in production. Everybody's shouting at everybody and last month one of my clients threatened to cancel next season's order because of delays in delivery.'** Sandra admits that while she interacts regularly with the cutter and the supervisor, she avoids contact with the machinists because she doesn't feel welcome on the factory floor: 'I just can't believe how much things have changed! We used to chat about work all the time and where we were going with the company. Now I don't even want to walk through their area. They seem to hate me.' **One of her most competent and experienced machinists resigned last month and Sandra's worried that others may follow**. She's hired you to help her sort out the problems.

Organizing the key facts/issues for yourself

To make sure that you don't miss out anything important and to help you think critically about the facts in the case, put them into a format that will help you with your analysis. Taking down notes from the case is also really important because it means that you're actively engaging with the content of the case – you're working with the information instead of just absorbing it passively. You could **list** the key facts or you could use a graphic organizer to **map** them for yourself.

Graphic organizers like mind maps can help you to stand back from the information in the case, group it, and see how the groups are connected – the same thing detectives do with their evidence boards (in the movies anyway!). Group the information in a way that makes sense to you and leave enough room to add notes as you think about the case.

It's time well spent because you start to see patterns and relationships that might have been hidden among all the information in the case. You can use different coloured pens to show relationships or highlight issues for yourself. And don't forget to indicate priority issues on your map or your list – I've indicated mine with bold lines in the map of the Moon Dust Designs context on the next page. You could also number them in order of priority.

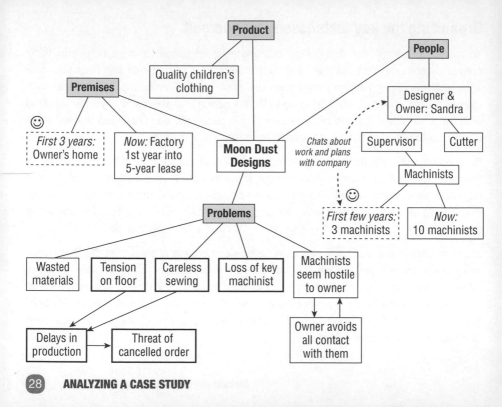

Product

Quality children's clothing

Premises

☺ First 3 years: Owner's home

Now: Factory 1st year into 5-year lease

Moon Dust Designs

People

Designer & Owner: Sandra

Chats about work and plans with company

Supervisor

Cutter

Machinists

☺ First few years: 3 machinists

Now: 10 machinists

Problems

Wasted materials

Tension on floor

Careless sewing

Loss of key machinist

Machinists seem hostile to owner

Delays in production

Threat of cancelled order

Owner avoids all contact with them

28   ANALYZING A CASE STUDY

Before you can start analysing the underlying causes of the problems, you need to make it clear for the reader which problems/issues in the case you're going to be analyzing and how you're going to do this. As explained on page 8 with the brief of the Moon Dust case, assignment briefs don't always define the nature of the problems to be addressed, so it's up to you to do this. This is usually done in the introduction to the assignment.

Provide a brief description of the context of the case, the problems/issues you'll be analyzing, and *how* you are going to be doing this. Don't describe the whole case in your introduction – your tutor generally already knows what's in it! If you're analyzing a case you've chosen yourself you'll need to include more detail about the individual/ organization in the case. If you're not sure how much detail to include, ask your tutor.

See *Report Writing* (Reid, 2012) in this series for advice on structuring the different sections of reports.

An example from the Moon Dust case:

Since the growth and relocation of the company to factory premises, the sewing process has been characterized by increasingly careless work practices, resulting in significant wastage of materials and delays in production, culminating in the recent threat of a cancelled order. Working relationships have deteriorated … and the loss of a key machinist.

The purpose of this report is to establish possible causes of the deterioration in working relationships and productivity in the company through an examination of current practices in the light of scholarly literature on … Following this analysis the report will provide recommendations aimed at restoring productive working relationships and practices in the company as soon as possible.

Provide a brief summary of the main symptoms of the problems in your own words.

Here the student describes the nature of the problems to be investigated – this is her own characterization of the symptoms and it will guide her analysis of the underlying causes. Later she will need to check that her recommended interventions do in fact address the underlying causes she identifies and can deliver on the promises set up in the aims of her report.

8 Interrogating the facts

Once you've identified the key facts in the case, you can start to open it up even more for analysis by taking a critical look at the facts. There are factors in the case that may not be explicitly stated. But if ideas pop into your head as you read, add them to your list or draw them onto your map.

Which evidence in the case suggests action is required?	Staff shouting at each other; quality of work deteriorating; serious delays in production; loss of key staff; owner reluctant to move around in her own premises.
Which factors could be contributing to the problem?	Sandra has hired you to sort out the problem with her staff. But are they the real source of the problem? Who are the other stakeholders in the organization? Are there any relationships that are missing? What about the environment of the organization? Could Sandra herself be part of the problem? Look at the wording of her comments carefully: 'We used to chat about the work all the time and where we were going with the company.' What does this suggest about the machinists' involvement in the company at that time? Sandra now describes the factory floor as 'their areas' – what does that tell you about her attitude? What has changed in the company since it grew larger?

Which key factors could potentially constrain (limit) the solution options?	Sandra has a five-year lease on the factory premises. Would there be legal and financial implications if she decided to outsource the production process to another company or another country?
Which factors could provide opportunities for the solution?	People who seem to be part of the problem may actually be key to its solution. The more experienced machinists at Moon Dust have skills that can help the other machinists if the right incentives are provided. So what kinds of incentives would these need to be?

Getting feedback on your ideas

Other students will have their own ideas about the case after reading it and they can be a valuable source of feedback for your own ideas. Many courses now also give you the opportunity to take part in online forum discussions on the assignment topics.

If you're working as part of a team[1] on a case, try to get together for a discussion as soon as possible after you've read the case so that you can discuss your ideas. Your

---

[1] Working in teams can be quite challenging so it's important to understand how to function effectively as part of a team. See *Success in Groupwork* (Hartley and Dawson, 2010) in this series for advice on effective teamwork.

tutors might give you time for these discussions in class but if they don't, make sure you plan meeting times at intervals throughout the project.

And later as you start to gather information from your readings, you're likely to shift the bits of information around even more and see other relationships or potential relationships in the case. As you read and think about the case, you start to make connections and shift things around.

One of the most frequently asked questions about case study assignments is what to do if there is missing information, and the answer will differ from assignment to assignment and course to course. Your cases mimic real-life work situations and many problem situations in your working life will present with missing details about the situation.

In some situations there'll be time to find the missing information; in others there won't, and then you'll have to make decisions about solutions based on the information you *do* have. This means that in some of your assignments, you will be expected to work within the limitations of the information provided in the case, and so you might be making a number of assumptions about the case. Any assumption must, however, be credible and justifiable, given the evidence in the case.

Part 3 will look more closely at working with the evidence in the case, but I'll just make the point here that you need to make it clear in your analysis that you are basing your conclusions about the case on the information you *do* have. One of the ways you can do this is by using hedging (tentative) language in referring to the case. See pages 63 and 76 for examples of assignments using hedging language to express levels of confidence/certainty about evidence from the case.

These are a few questions to consider when you feel there's information missing from a case:

1 Is the information available in your course guide?

  ▸ Some assignment briefs will include documents like internal letters, memos or emails to supplement the information in the case, so that you are collecting information from multiples sources – as you would do in real-life working situations.
  ▸ Some also include links to online interviews with key employees from the organization in the case or magazine articles about the organization.

References to these supplementary sources of information will often be included in the assignment brief. But when you're pushed for time and doing multiple assignments at once, it's easy to overlook details in assignment briefs.

2 Have you read the case closely enough?

Key information can be hidden in conversations or comments in the cases. Some cases will include tables and graphs with data that need to be read and interpreted or raw data to be processed.

3 Does the brief allow you to find more information on the case?

Sometimes, tutors will specify that you should *not* try to find more information on the case. For example, your tutors might use company cases from textbooks that contain information that is a few years old. Current company information might contradict the facts in the case and confuse the issues.

When should I *not* assume anything about the context?

Many cases feature very little information because your tutors *want* you to investigate the context of the situation for yourselves. The context is the building block for your

solution – if you don't have the relevant information, your solution is likely to fail. Many subjects will expect you to gather factual information about the context of cases.

For example, in engineering cases:

You can't design a roofing solution for a community without understanding the contextual factors that could constrain your design:

- *How big are their houses?*
- *What materials are used in the construction of their houses? This is crucial for understanding how heavy the roof can be.*
- *What are the climactic conditions of the region? You don't want your roof design to fail because you haven't made it strong enough to withstand the region's cyclonic winds.*

- *What is the average household income in the region? There's no point in designing a solution which no one can afford!*
- *What are the skills levels in the region? Someone's going to have to build your design!*

Some cases have so little contextual information that you need to construct the context for yourself through research. See page 80 for an example of the process required.

Where can I find missing background/contextual information?

The method you use to collect missing information will depend on the requirements of the assignment and what you're trying to find out. Some assignments might require you to:

▶ **Ask people in organizations:** When tutors want you to contact organizations outside the university, they will usually have permission from the organizations concerned for students to do this. Don't just turn up or phone and start firing off questions! If you are required to contact people, make sure that you prepare your questions well – you often have only one chance to ask them because people generally won't have much time to spend with you.

Remember that your analysis and recommendations will be made on the information you *do* have, so it's important to make this clear in your assignment.

▶ **Search for the information on the internet and in your library databases:** This is the most common requirement, especially at first-year level. Searching the internet for sources can be risky but your libraries have enormous collections of valuable and reliable background information and data. Knowing where to find it can save you a lot of time!

The best place to start is with the librarians who know most about finding information in your general area of study: subject librarians.

Subject librarians

Also sometimes known as **subject specialist librarians**, these are your best friends in the library! Ask about them at the front desk or find them on the library website – most library sites have prominent links to subject librarians.

Library
Search catalogue
Subject librarians
Subject guides
Article databases
Online tutorials
FAQs

Subject librarians have expertise and experience in providing services in specific subject areas. One of their most important roles in the library is to help students search for reliable sources for their assignments through:

- Email and Q&A links
- Online and face-to-face tutorials and consultations
- Course-specific workshops at the request of tutors – don't be tempted to skip these – they're well worth the time!

Subject librarians are also responsible for maintaining online **subject guides**, which provide useful starting points for finding both academic sources and also reliable non-academic sources of information and data.

Subject guides: finding non-academic information and data

You may be using this information for background to your case and also for the purpose of analysis. Subject guide sites **group** links to information and data to make them more easily accessible.

Sample groupings	Examples of links provided
Country profiles **Company profiles** **Market research reports**	Many libraries have licences to use **analytical reports** on local and international companies and markets, and country information. Example: SWOT analyses from Euromonitor International.
	Many libraries subscribe to **news databases**, which provide current news articles on companies, industries and financial markets. Example: Factiva.
Industry standards **Regulations** **Patents**	Your library is likely to provide links to **standards** for industries in your own country, e.g. nursing standards etc. If you're looking for industry standards in another country, you'll need to speak to the subject librarian.
Government	Government departments and their **policy documents** and **reports** on a wide range of issues, with useful **statistics** and links to related non-governmental organizations and agencies. Links to **parliamentary debates** and **legislation** in your country.
Organizations	**International organizations** such as the World Health Organization, which provides international health statistics and evidence-based guidelines, and **professional associations** such as the Institute of Electrical and Electronics Engineering.

ANALYZING THE CASE

Once you've identified all the key components of the case, you can start to analyze how they fit together to result in the current situation. You now need to move beyond the *symptom*s of the problem – the visible issues in the case – to the underlying *causes* of these problems and how these causes can be addressed. This is where you begin selecting information from your readings and applying it to the case. You want to make sure that your analysis of the case fits one of the main marking criteria for case study assignments, which usually reads something like this:

> Analysis makes appropriate and insightful connections between issues and problems in the case and relevant theory and research

Achieving this in your analysis means following a process of interrelated steps in which you need to:

- Select information that is appropriate to the case.
- Develop an argument in which you apply this information to issues in the case to provide your reader with informed and supported conclusions[1] about the issues/problems in the case.

This part takes you through this process, using examples from assignments to illustrate each step. The chapters are designed to stand on their own so that you can dip into bits that you need or you can read it as a whole. You'll see that all the way through we'll be moving between readings and the case, looking for links and making cross references. The first step is selecting relevant readings, but in order to do that efficiently, we need to discuss exactly what you'll be looking for in the readings …

---

[1] I'm indebted to Ellet (2007) for the idea that arguments in a case study assignment consist of a series of evidence-based conclusions about the case.

- Is the organization/individual in the case doing what the literature says they should be doing? Why? Why not? You'll be explaining by *applying* what the readings say to the issues/events in the case.
- How could this be contributing to the situation described in the case? What is the *real* problem(s) underlying the issues described in the case?
- How can the organization/individual in the case change what they're doing to fit best practice as described in the readings?

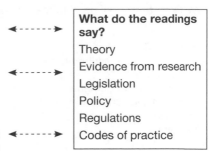

What do the readings say?
Theory
Evidence from research
Legislation
Policy
Regulations
Codes of practice

Best practice can be described as practice that has been shown to work well – sometimes known as **evidence-based practice**. See Chapter 14 for a discussion of best practice and moving further to best *fit* practice for the organization.

11 Selecting relevant readings

Your tutor may have given you a list of recommended readings specifically for the assignment, but generally you'll be starting with a combination of your lecture notes and your reading list for the module. Your reading list provides a solid starting point but it's likely that you'll need to read beyond this as well.

READING LIST
- Chapters from prescribed book
- Journal articles
- Links to policy documents, industry regulations/guidelines
- News items
- Video links

Consider:
Why has this reading been included?
Does it look relevant to the case?

Keep your case and case notes in front of you all the time so that your selection of readings is focused on the case. Some of the items in the reading list may be relevant to the case, others not – it's up to you to judge using the Table of Contents in books, abstracts of journal articles, summaries and so on. Take control of the reading list as soon as you can – or it can start to control you and it's easy to lose sight of the case in all the readings. See *Reading and Making Notes* (Godfrey, 2014) in this series for advice on reading lists and moving beyond these lists – finding additional sources.

Sample reading list entries

Below is an extract from the reading list for a nursing module: Health and Well-Being for the Older Adult. In their first assignment in this module, students are required to view a video showing an interaction between a nurse and an older adult patient in a nursing home and identify possible causes for the patient's reluctance to share information with the nurse.

On the reading list	Does it look relevant to the case?
Taylor S P et al. (2013) Cross-cultural communication barriers in health care. *Nursing Standard*, 27(31): 35–43.	Culture is always a vital consideration in any case and is mentioned specifically in the codes of practice of health organizations around the world. Do the nurse and patient in the case have different cultural backgrounds? Is this stated explicitly in the case? Are there clues on the patient's bedside table that the nurse should be noticing?

Williams K, Kemper S and Hummert M L (2004) Enhancing communication with older adults: Overcoming elderspeak. *Journal of Gerontological Nursing*, 30(10): 17–25.	The word 'overcoming' in the subtitle seems to suggest that this article looks at a specific problem involved in communication with older adults: elderspeak. Any evidence of the problem in the case? Does the article provide suggestions for preventing it? Evidence of solutions that work? Any other articles or book chapters that mention it? Was it covered in lectures?

On page 49 we look at a paragraph using these sources to present an argument about the possible causes of the problem in the nursing case. But before we do that, some advice on applying theory and research to a case …

Developing an argument in a case study assignment

Your tutors don't want long descriptions of either the readings or the case – they want the two brought together all through the analysis. You're going to be presenting an argument about the case using the readings – **your voice** is going to guide the analysis.

Imagine yourself as a lawyer in court. What would the judge think if you simply read out all the facts of the case, then presented a long list of evidence you've gathered, without explaining the connection between the facts and the evidence, and without presenting an argument about the implications for the case?

How do I make sure I'm presenting clear arguments about the case?

Each paragraph should present one main argument about your interpretation of the case – one main conclusion you've come to after weighing up the evidence in the case (conversations/actions) against what you found in the literature.

The paragraph on the next two pages provides an argument from the nursing case study, which required students to identify possible reasons why the older adult patient in the case could be reluctant to share information with the nurse in the case, thus jeopardizing his care. References to theory and research are highlighted in the paragraph to help you see the movement between case and readings.

Notice how the student brings together evidence from the case and the literature to identify one possible underlying cause of this problem. To support her conclusion that this is a possible cause, she provides a **critical examination** of the nurse's words and actions in the case **in the light of theory and research** on communication with older adult patients.

One possible cause of the patient's reluctance to share information with the nurse in the case is the nurse's use of elderspeak in communicating with him. Elderspeak, also known as 'baby talk' or 'infantilizing speech' is an over-accommodating speech style used by younger carers to communicate with older adults whom they often assume to be incapable of following normal speech patterns (Williams et al. 2004). The nurse's verbal communication with the patient features a number of characteristics of elderspeak. For example, on first walking into the room the nurse uses a tag question: 'You're getting cold in here with that window open, aren't you?' instead of the direct 'Are you getting cold with the window open?' The use of this indirect communication implies that the patient is not competent to understand the question and make independent choices (Williams 2009). …

Topic sentence presenting main argument. Identifies conclusion drawn from comparison of nurse's communication with patient and problematic practice described in the literature as <u>elderspeak</u>.

Explanation/definition of the term used in the topic sentence.

Application to the case with reference to specific facts or events in the case as evidence of the practice, including the quoted words of the nurse.

Explanation drawn from the literature about why this practice is a problem. Provides support to main argument in the paragraph.

… This attitude towards the patient is reinforced by the fact that the nurse does not wait for his response before closing the window. She also uses inappropriate endearments throughout the conversation, calling the patient 'Sweetie' rather than referring to him by his name and using a higher pitch of voice and slowed speech, all behaviours characteristic of elderspeak (Williams 2009). While the nurse's intention with this style of speech might be to express a caring and compassionate attitude, and put the patient at ease, many older adults find elderspeak patronizing and demeaning (Kemper and Harden 1999) and this can alienate them from the carer (Hart 2010) and inhibit their disclosure of information and concerns.

Further evidence of elderspeak in the case. Notice that this is not just a repetition of the facts of the case – the student is interpreting the actions of the nurse in the light of the theory.

Evidence from research supporting the theoretical argument that elderspeak can present a barrier to information sharing by older adults. Notice how this argument takes us back to the first sentence of the paragraph.

So, in linking the case with theory and research, the student draws **reasonable conclusions (inferences)** about how the nurse's behaviour could be contributing to the problem in the case.

How do I know I'm analyzing instead of just describing the case in my paragraphs?

How many sentences have you devoted to the case alone? Try shading your text as I've done in the example. If you have big chunks of information from the case with no reference to theoretical concepts or research, it's likely that you're just describing it. Be very careful that you're not simply telling the story of what's happened in the case or repeating the facts.

Marking guidelines for case study assignments usually make quite clear reference to this issue:

You want to be here ...	Not here ...
Provides a balanced, critical examination of the facts in the case in light of relevant theory and research to provide well-supported conclusions about underlying causes of issues identified in the case and how these can be addressed.	Simply repeats the facts of the case without discussing the relevance of these facts to the issues in the case and provides no attempt at critical analysis.

See *Getting Critical* (Williams, 2014) in this series for advice on providing critical analysis in assignments.

To help you get there, Chapter 13 looks at the nuts and bolts of case analysis – the work that lies behind producing sound, well-supported insights into a case. This starts with using tools and critical frameworks for your note taking, beginning with diagnosing underlying problems.

13 Diagnosing underlying causes of problems

How often have you heard people talk about 'getting to the *root* of the problem'? This is an acknowledgement of the fact that many problem situations in life are complex and require a lot of digging around before we can identify the underlying or root causes. Notice I use the word **causes** in the plural form here because there are often several causes to problems.

Some of them may be quite near the surface and others may be buried a lot deeper in systems and relationships in the organization.

Avoiding premature judgements

Premature judgements about problems often involve isolating and blaming someone.

If a maintenance worker uses the incorrect ladder for a particular job and falls and breaks his leg, then it's his fault for not following procedure. If there's a problem with workplace bullying – find the bullies and get rid of them. Problem solved!

Really? **Why** did the bullying go on for as long as it did? What enabled or maybe even encouraged the behaviour of the bullies in the first place? **Why** wasn't the maintenance worker following correct procedure? Did he understand the correct procedure properly?

Effective and lasting solutions lie in addressing the problems within the system that can lead to failures by individuals or groups within that system. If organizations don't sort out the underlying causes of problems, these problems will simply occur again and again.

Our nurse in the elderspeak case is using elderspeak, which could be an underlying factor in the patient's reluctance to communicate with her. And it certainly needs to be addressed as a cause in the case. But **why** is she doing this? Is there any policy about communicating with patients? Training provided?

Digging down

The causes for problems are often a complex mix of issues with individual people and organizational systems. This is why your cases are so full of details – they present you with the systems in which problems or incidents occur in real life. Case study analysis can include digging into a wide variety of systems – country, school, company, family and individual – to find underlying causes to problems.

The key to finding these causes is asking **why**. **Why is this happening?** And you'll be using your coursework to help you answer this.

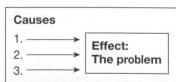

But when you've got an enormous amount of detail to dig through in a case and in the literature, it's really useful to be able to organize the possible causes for yourself in some way. There are lots of cause–effect graphic organizers you can use to help you with this.

One cause-effect organizer that can be particularly useful for brainstorming in case study analysis is a **fishbone diagram**[1] because it allows you to categorize possible causes using elements of the system presented in your case. This is a tool that is commonly used for brainstorming possible causes for problems in the workplace and since you're looking at cases mimicking situations in the workplace, it makes sense to use the same tools!

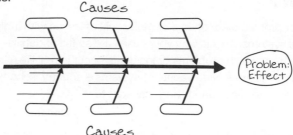

---

[1] Also called an Ishikawa diagram after its inventor Professor Kaoru Ishikawa. The sketches used here are the author's own interpretation of the tool.

Fishbone diagrams: how they work

The problem or **effect** is placed at the head of the fish along the backbone. Possible contributing factors you've identified in the case are listed as the smaller bones under categories of **causes**, which you choose yourself.

Examples of categories often used for this are:

Fishbone diagrams can be adapted to any case situation you like. For example, it's easy to see how you could include the 4 Ps of marketing as categories.

These diagrams are often used in workplaces when staff have a clearly identified problem to investigate (e.g. long waiting times for patients at hospitals) and lots of causal factors present at the same time. In these cases people representing the whole system in the workplace (the main stakeholders) get together – doctors, nurses, administrators and reception staff (and patient feedback in the form of surveys). They brainstorm the causes of the delays by contributing information from their particular perspectives. This gives the group a systematic way of noting down ideas and a visual picture of causes and relationships between them in the system as a whole.

In your case studies the stakeholders and their perspectives are assembled on the pages of the case or in the video you need to watch. And you're matching these with theory and research from your readings. When you don't have a specific theoretical framework to guide you, the categories commonly used in fishbone diagrams can provide a system for jotting down ideas as you read about them in the literature and start making connections with the case:

▶ What does the literature say about *where* the causes of the kind of problem in the case are commonly located?

▶ Can you find evidence of this in the case? What do you need to investigate further?

Let's break it down a bit using some categories that could be used and then we'll look at an example of how this information can be placed on a fishbone diagram or used however you like! The table below provides a few commonly used categories of information to start looking for causes of problems:

Possible categories of causes: What does the literature say?	Any evidence of these factors in the case?
People: Is the problem commonly located in people who lack specific knowledge? Are not prepared to share their knowledge? Refuse to acquire new knowledge? Specific personalities?	Comments? Conversations?
Procedures: Is the problem often caused by staff who are not properly trained or not trained at all? Are there certain procedures that should be followed in this type of workplace/situation?	Arguments? Descriptions? Documents? Events?
Policy: Is a lack of policy often a problem? A lack of clarity on policy? A lack of buy-in from staff on policies? A lack of training on implementing policies?	Indications of any unofficial policies, mottos or practices in the organization?
Company/organization: Do they sometimes/often place a low priority on issues that can lead to this problem? Are they sometimes not sufficiently aware of this problem? Are they constantly cutting costs? Taking risks?	*Remember: You're looking at making inferences from what's said or done in the case. People might not actually use the word 'policy' in a comment but you could still come to a conclusion about company policy (official/unofficial) from what speakers say and who they are.*
Environment: Does the presence of specific environmental factors often contribute to this problem? Example: constant stress; pressure for performance; uncertainty about future of jobs; a culture of acceptance of unsafe or uncivil behaviour.	

Possible categories of causes: What does the literature say?	Any evidence of these factors in the case?
Equipment: Is there certain equipment that should be used in this kind of situation? If it's not being used or not being used correctly, can it give rise to the kind of problem in the case?	*Sift through the details of the case very carefully.*

On page 62 you'll find a brief extract from a student's brainstorming notes for an assignment on workplace bullying – note the connections to theory and research and the possible links made from section to section. This will be followed by extracts from an answer to the assignment, with some advice on presenting arguments showing cause and effect.

A bit of information from the case first:

Case: Large insurance sales company

The new head of HR is concerned after the resignation of valuable staff member Jason. Jason's exit interview detailed serious and ongoing verbal abuse by team leader (Tina) and a failure by Tina's manager (Dale) to intervene after Jason reported it, followed by rapidly escalating bullying, which culminated in Jason's hospitalization for depression and his resignation.

The head of HR has uncovered other similar cases, one of them involving Tina, and is worried about the potential for legal action against the company. He's asked you to find out why bullying allegations in the company are not properly investigated, and always seem to result in the victims resigning while alleged bullies never seem to face any consequences, even though the company has a specific anti-bullying policy in place.

Manager (Dale): Called Tina in for meeting and told her to 'tone down' the comments. Didn't enquire further or monitor situation: 'It didn't seem that serious to be honest!'

Team leader and bully (Tina): Very good at getting results from team. Promoted despite previous allegation of bullying against her. Says teasing helps team 'let off steam' in pressured environment and claims Jason 'overreacted'.

Team member (Patrick): Knew Tina often went 'way, way too far' with jokes about Jason's personal life and humiliating pranks played on him but went along because he didn't want to be 'labelled a troublemaker' in the company and targeted himself.

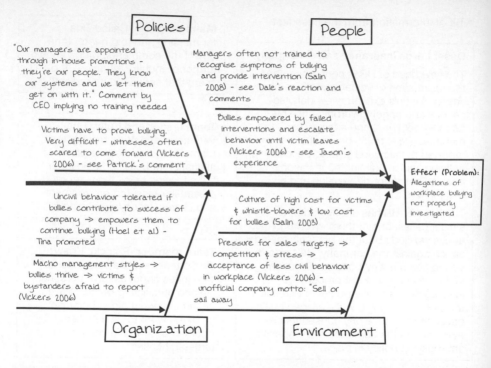

Policies

"Our managers are appointed through in-house promotions - they're our people. They know our systems and we let them get on with it." Comment by CEO implying no training needed

Victims have to prove bullying. Very difficult - witnesses often scared to come forward (Vickers 2006) - see Patrick's comment

People

Managers often not trained to recognise symptoms of bullying and provide intervention (Salin 2008) - see Dale's reaction and comments

Bullies empowered by failed interventions and escalate behaviour until victim leaves (Vickers 2006) - see Jason's experience

Effect (Problem): Allegations of workplace bullying not properly investigated

Uncivil behaviour tolerated if bullies contribute to success of company → empowers them to continue bullying (Hoel et al) - Tina promoted

Macho management styles → bullies thrive → victims & bystanders afraid to report (Vickers 2006)

Culture of high cost for victims & whistle-blowers & low cost for bullies (Salin 2003)

Pressure for sales targets → competition & stress → acceptance of less civil behaviour in workplace (Vickers 2006) - unofficial company motto: "Sell or sail away

Organization

Environment

Writing about cause and effect

From an answer to the workplace bullying assignment:

One possible contributing factor to the lack of resolution in bullying cases is that managers in the company are not trained to recognize possible signs of bullying and provide appropriate and timely intervention. Manager Dale's acceptance of the explanation that Jason 'totally overreacted to a few in-group jokes' suggests that he is unaware of the potential for interpersonal jokes and banter to escalate into verbal and even physical bullying when the victim objects to the behaviour (Salin 2003). As a result he fails to investigate further or monitor the situation after his meeting with the team leader: 'I thought Tina would take care of it' ...

Cause indicated by 'contributing factor'. **Effect** indicated by 'As a result' See Manchester University's *Academic Phrasebank* (2015) for phrases to indicate cause and effect in situations.

Evidence from case to support conclusion that managers are not trained on bullying issues. Note the tentative language here – 'suggests' – the student is indicating that evidence from the case has led her to this conclusion – she's not stating it as a fact. This use of tentative language is known as *hedging*. In the first sentence she also refers to *one possible factor* – she's looking at only a single case in the company so she's not claiming this definitely *is* a cause.

Failure to intervene in reported bullying cases could also be reinforcing bullying behaviour in the organization and discouraging witnesses from coming forward with evidence. Salin (2008) argues that when organizations fail to address allegations of bullying, this can create a culture of low costs for bullying behaviour and high costs for reporting this behaviour. Patrick's comment that he was afraid to be labelled a 'troublemaker' …

Notice how the cause discussed in the second paragraph (Failure to intervene) links with the cause discussed in the paragraph before. Problems in cases often have a number of interlinking causes and you can indicate this relationship in the topic sentences of your paragraphs.

Can you spot the hedging in this paragraph?

Keeping up with names in cases

When cases feature a lot of different people (as the bullying case above does), it's important to be consistent in how you refer to the people in the case.

If you've been calling characters by their names and then want to refer to their positions in their organizations, you can add information:

> 'As CEO of the company, Mike is responsible for …'
> 'In his capacity as CEO, Mike has the authority to …'

Making the links between theory and case

You'll be moving between coursework and case all the time in your investigation, using the theory you learn in the course as the critical lens through which you're viewing the case.

One of the things that can make this really tricky is that cases are not written using the terms and concepts found in your lecture notes and books; conversations and events are not categorized into theoretical concepts – they're described in the everyday language of real life. This is done on purpose because this is what you'll be encountering in the workplace where situations are not neatly sewn up and packaged in an easy-to-access format.

So how do you start matching theory to the case? There's really no magic answer to this – it's a process of looking through the theory and going back to the case, and then back to the theory and back to the case, until you start picking up clues and seeing match-ups between the two.

On the next page I've included two sample lecture slides with some comments showing a thinking process about how the materials featured could be applied to the Moon Dust case. You can't generally use lecture notes as sources in your assignments but they give you an overview of the course material – the big picture – and they can guide you towards readings on the topic. Go back to page 28 for a quick reminder of the facts in the case and then come back here for a demonstration of how to:

Follow the clues ... find the readings ... make the connections ... draw your conclusions

Course material: What does it say? How can this be applied to the case?

Effective internal feedback

Advice, support, critique
- Positive & negative
- Formal or informal
- Downwards & upwards:
  Superior
  ↕
  Subordinate
  Between peers

Functions:
Inform;
correct;
reward;
lead to
better things

(Eunson 2008)

Employee participation

Involvement of staff at some level in:
- Planning
- Decision making
- Goal setting
- Performance monitoring

Effective feedback systems
key to success

(Hannagan 2008)

The word 'feedback' isn't used in the case but isn't that what the supervisor's actually doing and the machinists between themselves? Not effective though – seems to be negative only and causing conflict. Also isn't correcting, rewarding (**Link to motivation there??**) or leading to better things. Good framework to compare with practice in company.

What about Sandra – is she giving any feedback? She says she used to chat to the machinists all the time – informal feedback there? Were the machinists feeding back to her too? She says they used to 'chat about the work all the time' and 'where **we** were going with the company' **Employee participation at that time?**

Does she get any feedback from them now? Unlikely – she doesn't go into their areas at all. Definitely need to look into this further: remember the title of the case – 'Crossing the Floor'. Could this be part of where she's going wrong now – a clue to the solution? Do the machinists need to be more involved?

Follow the clues … find the readings … make the connections … draw your conclusions

Using a critical framework to take notes from readings: answering the *why* questions

Keep a clear record of what you find in the readings and where you found it, so that you have easy access to the information when you need it to write up your assignment. Note dates and page numbers where you found information to avoid having to go back and find it again. And to make sure that you are keeping your eye on the need to explain **why** something is a problem (what effect can it have?), you can add **why** questions to your notes as I've done on the next page.

I've used another note-taking format – this time a table format for the notes on the next page so that I could lay out a few of the multiple causes I've identified together with comparison of best practice in readings (and the **why** answers for both), with references to theory in the middle. You'll notice as you take your notes that the issues are often interrelated (as we saw in the bullying case).

In your assignment you'll be using the theoretical concepts to arrange and develop your arguments.

Symptoms	Underlying cause? (and effects)	Best practice: What *should* the organisation be doing?	Theory/ research
Shouting on factory floor	Lack of effective feedback systems and training ↓	Regular, goal-directed feedback based on shared objectives	Feedback (Eunson 2008)
Waste of materials	**Why is this a problem?** – Random, reactive feedback practices – Focus on problems only – No reward for good work ↓	**Why is this important?** – solution-focused problem solving – clarity of task requirements and roles	Teamwork (West 2012)
Careless sewing	Communication breakdowns Demotivating environment ↓	Performance linked reward structures (money/ promotion)	Equity theory (Adams 1963)
Perceived hostility to owner	Attitude of 'they don't care so why should we?' Perceptions of unfairness ↓	**Why is this important?** – fulfils need for recognition of achievement & fairness – can motivate to perform	Motivation (Hannagan 2008)
Loss of key staff	Lack of job satisfaction	– links to job satisfaction & staff retention	

Symptoms	Underlying cause? (and effects)	Best practice: What *should* the organisation be doing?	Theory/research
Shouting on factory floor *Waste of materials* *Careless sewing* *Perceived hostility to owner* *Loss of key staff*	Shift from participative management practices ↓ **Why is this a problem?** Loss of upward–downward consultation between machinists & owner ↓ Development of 'Us and them' culture ↓ Atmosphere of mutual distrust	Employee participation in operational goal-setting, decision making & problem solving **Why is this important?** – sense of partnership in working towards shared goals – feeling of being valued for contribution – greater job satisfaction and staff retention	Employee participation (Hannagan 2008) Research (Gennard and Judge 2005)

Drawing conclusions from the case: expressing levels of certainty

In drawing your conclusions you'll be expressing varying levels of certainty or confidence – depending on the **strength** of evidence in the case in light of theory and research on the topic.

3 Employee involvement and participation

3.1 Shift from participative management practices

The owner's comment that when the company was much smaller 'we used to chat about the work all the time and where we were going with the company' suggests that at that time the company functioned as an effective team in which the owner collaborated with the machinists on operational issues, and involved them in future planning and goal setting for the company. Involvement of employees in this way helps to establish a culture of partnership in the organization (Hannagan 2008). In this situation employees are more likely to feel valued for their contribution to the organization and to experience higher levels of job satisfaction, motivation, commitment and organizational trust (Gennard and Judge 2005, cited in Hannagan 2008). In contrast, the current perceived hostility of the machinists towards the owner could be indicative of a divisive 'us and them' culture which has developed with the rapid growth of the company and subsequent loss of upward–downward communication between the owner and the machinists …

Strength of evidence from case
The use of 'suggests' in this first sentence indicates that the writer is fairly confident about the conclusion drawn from evidence in the case.

Strength of evidence from case
The use of 'could be indicative' in this sentence means that the writer is *slightly* less confident about this conclusion but there is still sufficient evidence to support it. She now needs to explain further. Notice also that the student refers to the 'perceived' hostility of the machinists to indicate that this is the owner's perception of the situation – rather than an established fact.

In the assignment extract we've just seen, current practice in the case is being compared with what the literature says is the most effective way of doing things. The student is drawing conclusions about how the owner's current practice is contributing to the problems in the case by comparing what she *is* doing with what the literature says she *should be* doing (or in this case, should have continued doing). In your case study assignments, you're going to be referring to best practice in discussing the underlying causes of problems in the cases as well as possible solutions.

Best practice refers to what is accepted as being the most effective way of doing things in specific situations. This is generally informed by *evidence* that these practices work well. In your case study assignments, what is seen as best practice can depend on a number of factors such as:

▶ The specific industry or profession you'll be working in – many have their own guidelines or codes of practice and you'll be referring to these in analyzing problems and designing solutions.

▶ The theoretical models being used for the analysis of the situation.

It's important to remember that the literature doesn't always agree about what constitutes best practice and when something is put forward as best practice, you'll notice that the researchers will almost always discuss the **limitations** or potential disadvantages associated with this practice. The same is expected of you in your case study assignments.

Going back to our nursing case on page 49, the student could follow up her paragraph about the inappropriate use of elderspeak in the case with discussion of appropriate best practice techniques that can be used to put the patient at ease:

The nurse can use a number of effective non-verbal communication techniques to put the patient at ease. One of these is the use of open body language (Balzar-Riley 2008). For example, Doherty and Thompson (2014) suggest that sitting at the same height as the patient, leaning slightly towards him and maintaining comfortable eye contact can convey the message that the nurse is relaxed in the situation. This in turn helps to relax the patient. Doherty and Thompson caution however that the use of non-verbal cues such as eye contact and proximity to the patient may be inappropriate and even offensive to patients with certain religious and cultural beliefs. The setting in the case shows no overt signs of any religious or cultural affiliations …

This discussion shows awareness of how crucial it is to take the context of the case into account when considering best practice and solutions for any problem. Always show critical awareness of best practice – would it suit the context of the case? Any strong religious or cultural affiliation could offer constraints or opportunities for the solution. See page 45 for discussion of these considerations. We're looking at best practice first, but in evaluating solutions in Part 4, we'll look at 'best fit' practice – what will fit the **context** of the case best.

Framing an analysis using a specified theoretical framework

On the next page is an extended extract from an answer to the assignment on a child's aggressive behaviour (see page 9). This extract uses a specific theoretical model (ecological systems theory) as its framework for analysis and another, related theory, in support. Notice how the student integrates the theories with evidence from the case and the research to draw conclusions about causal factors of the child's behaviour – sometimes tentative and sometimes stronger conclusions.

Comments are provided on how the student has indicated levels of certainty about evidence in the case and links with the literature.

A central aspect of the theory (ecological theory) is *briefly* introduced with a statement of links to possible causes of behaviour.

Microsystem

Some of the most direct influences on a child's behaviour can be found in the child's participation in interactions with individuals or groups within immediate environments such as the home and school (Hong and Espalage 2012).

The social worker's record of inter-parental violence in Dylan's home and his father's comment to the headmaster that Dylan was 'punched around all the time by his older brothers until he grew a backbone and learned to fight back' would seem to indicate that Dylan has experienced high rates of aggression and coercive exchanges within the home environment. These conditions are often associated with the development of aggressive behaviour in children (Ensor et al. 2010; Kauffman and Landram 2013).

Evidence from the case is provided, including a document and comments by a central stakeholder in the case – Dylan's father. The student draws a conclusion about this evidence and then links it to research.

Strength of evidence from case: In this first sentence the phrase 'would seem to indicate' suggests a fairly high level of confidence about this conclusion and the evidence in the case certainly seems to support this.

Social learning theory (Bandura 1997), which also emphasizes the reciprocal influence of environmental factors on behaviour development, offers a possible explanation for Dylan's aggression in the classroom setting. Social learning suggests that children learn aggressive behaviour through observation of the direct consequences of aggressive or non-aggressive acts in their social environments (Kauffman and Landram 2013). It is possible that Dylan has learned that aggression is a legitimate way of resolving interpersonal conflict and is now using this strategy with his peers in the classroom …

Moving towards solutions: making the connections

Your identification of possible underlying causal factors in the case should lead logically to related solutions. So, for example, if Dylan's family, his peers and his teachers are part of the problem, then they should all be part of the solution. If you are using the argument that Dylan's behaviour is *learned* behaviour, then you are likely to be recommending interventions based on *learning* new behaviour.

You'll be using your readings to develop possible solution ideas:

- What works well in these kinds of situations?
- Why does it work?
- Can you find evidence/examples of where it has worked before?
- What are the limitations and costs of this kind of solution?

And then, very importantly:

- Would this kind of solution fit the case?

In the Moon Dust case, for example, the owner won't be able to interact with all the machinists to the same extent that she did before the growth of the company (see the notes on page 31) because there are a lot more of them and she has far more work now. So you'd need to find a solution that still engages the machinists in a productive partnership with the owner but which fits the current context.

However, before you start developing your solution ideas, go back to your notes on the context of the case – the key components.

Reassemble the components of the case for yourself

Before you start looking at possible solutions, it's a good idea to reassemble all the stakeholders in the case and all the facts of the case – go back to your evidence board with the insight your cause–effect analysis has given you and start to consider possible solutions. Shift the components around with the new insight given to you by your cause–effect analysis.

▶ What do the stakeholders need or need to *do* to change the situation from problem situation to desired situation?
▶ Who will be involved in the solution and what will be their role in bringing it about?
▶ Who might no longer be there in your solution (in the long run or immediately)?

Some assignments require students to list the key stakeholders and their specific needs before beginning the discussion of the solution process. From this they then draw up a list of design requirements for their solution and later evaluate their proposed solutions against this list of requirements. Even if you don't need to provide a list of stakeholder needs and design requirements, it's not a bad idea to take the time to make a list of these for yourself to make sure that your solution is grounded in the needs of the stakeholders (as identified by your analysis) and the constraints and opportunities presented by the realities of the situation.

This is particularly important when the case provides very little contextual detail and you have to find it all yourself.

Solutions for cases with few details

Some cases provide so little contextual information that you have to build it yourself. For example, students in the health and medical sciences might be given a brief that reads:

Write an essay in which you discuss post-surgical pain assessment and intervention for a five year old male appendectomy patient.

The details of this case will need to be constructed from current research on:

| The condition | What causes it? Are there other conditions/problems (physical and emotional) commonly associated with it? |
| The surgical procedure | What is the location and source of the pain your patient is likely to be experiencing? |

| The patient
– Age group
– Gender | Is the patient likely to be **able** to report on pain levels and experience? Why? Levels of parental support needed?
Is he likely to be **willing** to report on his pain? Why? Potential cultural issues? |
| Available assessment procedures and interventions
(Your solution) | Which procedures would best suit *this* patient?
What could indicate or contraindicate particular interventions? Why?
Who else should be present during interventions? |

Check your assignment brief for any specifications about evidence from research:

▸ How current does it need to be?
▸ What kind of research is required?

So you've pulled apart the case to find the underlying causes of the problems. Your analysis showed there's a better way of doing things – so how do you put the parts back together again to build a solution? This is the beginning of the decision-making process: now you're going translate your theoretical consideration of best practice to practical solutions – *actions* that could be taken to move the situation from what it is now (problem situation) to where you want it to be (desired situation).

Some examples from the Moon Dust case:

Situation now: Underlying problems	Actions to be taken?	Desired situation through best practice
No upward–downward consultation between machinists and owner: 'Us and them' culture		Employee participation in goal setting, problem solving and operational decision processes
Lack of any recognition or reward for good performance by machinists	**Context of case:** Who? What? Where? When? How? Why?	Reward for performance which – is equitable (fair and just) – satisfies individual needs

A good way to start is to think about all the possible solutions you can – brainstorm the solution.

Brainstorming techniques

If you're working on your own, jot down all the ideas that come to mind. Make sure you record them as soon as they occur to you – it's really easy to forget lightbulb moments! Don't worry about reality checks or getting your ideas into any sort of order at this point – just get them down. Your ideas could involve both:

▸ Improving existing systems by making changes.
▸ Replacing existing systems with something completely new (innovation).

This is the creative phase of the problem-solving process so don't hold back! Later, you'll become critical and start narrowing down the solutions and finally select one. But for now let the ideas flow.

If you're working in a group, appoint someone as a scribe to note down all the ideas on a board or a large sheet of paper. Make sure that no one interrupts the flow of ideas with evaluative comments like 'But hold on, that won't work because …'. It's crucial to avoid reality checks at this point because that will stifle creativity and can make people in the group reluctant to present their ideas.

You also don't have to be in the same room as your group to collaborate on solutions. Google Docs can be used to brainstorm ideas (and later refine your chosen solution). You can create a single Google Doc for the group to work on and everyone adds their ideas, images and so on. Group members who might be reluctant to contribute ideas in public may be more willing to do so online, which might seem a little less risky to them. The same rules should apply though – don't add any evaluative comments until all the suggestions are in.

Before you begin the process of brainstorming and selecting solutions, go back to your brief. Your solutions must be aligned with the requirements and it's easy to forget about these in the race to solutions!

PART 4

SELECTING A SOLUTION

There's often no single best solution for case study assignments. What your marker generally wants to see is that you can suggest appropriate solutions that address the underlying problems in the case, and that you can justify these solutions.

This means that you are going to be evaluating the strengths and limitations of your solution options in terms of the literature on the topic and also the realities of the organization/group or individual in the case – the context of the case. Many case study assignments will require that you evaluate at least two or three possible solutions for the problems in the case.

Many cases will require improvement as well as **replacement** of existing systems. In the Moon Dust case, for example, this could include:

- Formulating a shared mission statement, objectives and expectations for the organization
- Establishing a system of staff representation and scheduled meetings with owner
- Placing suggestion boxes in communal staff areas
- Providing regular on-the job training at working on interdependent tasks
- Establishing a financial incentive scheme based on performance objectives
- **Redesigning the machinists' work by establishing self-managed work teams headed by the most competent machinists.**

Notice that these are all *actions* to be taken. And all solutions you put forward must be critically analysed for the reader.

Make sure you're here ...	Not here ...
Presents a number of feasible solution options that address the main issues in the case and critically analyzes these options with reference to the literature and the context of the case.	Few, if any, feasible solution options are presented and these are described only and not supported by critical analysis.

Critical analysis of solution options involves addressing a number of questions:

- How would your solutions work to address the problems in the case?
- Do you have evidence of where they have worked before in comparable situations?
- What are the limitations of the solution options?
- How could these limitations be controlled?

Some cases will require a combination of solutions to address immediate needs and facilitate long term solutions. In other cases you might be evaluating a number of solutions against a set of criteria and selecting the best one. We're going to look at notes for a critical analysis of two of the solutions for the Moon Dust case and a decision matrix for an engineering case.

Let's start with the Moon Dust case:

Solution	Critical analysis of solution	Theory/research
Establish financial incentive scheme based on performance objectives	**Why could it work?** Rewards performance → motivation	Expectancy theory (Vroom 1964)
	Potential limitation? Not everyone motivated by financial gain	Two-factor theory (Hertzberg 1997)
Redesign the machinists' work by establishing self-managed work teams headed by the most competent machinists and reporting directly to owner	**Why could it work?** Immediate feedback and coaching in teams.	Teamwork (West 2012)
	Responsibility and degree of autonomy in operational planning, decision making and monitoring of performance → greater job satisfaction and productivity	Job characteristics model (Hackman and Oldham 1975)
	Creates path for advancement for key staff and satisfies need for recognition of achievement → motivation and retention	Two-factor theory (Hertzberg 1997)
	Evidence of where it has worked? Meta-analysis of 131 studies of organizational change found introduction of autonomous and semi-autonomous teams had greatest effect on overall firm performance	Research (Macy and Izumi cited in West 2012)
	Potential limitation? Staff currently don't trust owner → might question motives and be reluctant to accept change. Owner needs to reopen channels of communication and acknowledge mistakes	Trust repair (Gillespie and Dietz 2009)

Using a decision matrix

Teams of engineering students will often use a decision matrix at various points in their development of solutions for cases. One of these points is to weigh up solution options designed by different members of the team against selection criteria reflecting the needs of the stakeholders in the case – the key people who are going to be constructing and using their solutions. The team scores the different solution options against the criteria, and selects the solution options with the highest score. So, for example, a decision for a roofing solution might look something like this:

Decision matrix

Selection criteria	Solution 1	Solution 2	Solution 3	Solution 4
Size				
Affordability				
Aesthetic appeal				
Ease of installation				
Ease of maintenance				
Total				

Always consider the context:

Factors	A few considerations for the context
Time	How long will your solutions take to implement? How soon do the solutions need to start working for the organization? Do you have short-term as well as long-term solutions? For example, setting up self-managed work teams for Moon Dust Designs will be a fairly lengthy process if it's done properly. It's likely that this will need to be a longer term solution option. The owner needs to complement this with actions that will work more quickly. See pages 92–93 for an example.
Cost	How much will the solution cost to implement? How much does the client have available to spend at this time?
Knowledge/ skills required	Does the organization/group/individual currently have the skills to implement your solutions? If not, how much will it cost (time and money) to acquire these skills?
Materials	What materials are required for your solution? Will these need to be bought? What will they cost? Or are they freely available in the environment of the case?
Legislation/ practice codes or standards	Will the implementation of your solution require any form of legal advice or support? How much will this cost? Could your solution possibly breach any guidelines or industry standards?

Effect on key stakeholders	Would your solution meet the needs of all the key stakeholders in the group? If you're focusing on a particular group of stakeholders, how would your solution affect other stakeholders in the organization? Will the key stakeholders be willing to accept the solution? For example, how would the supervisor in the Moon Dust case feel about self-managed groups? Would she resist this change because it might undermine her authority or make her insecure about her job? Is her role even necessary with this change? Make sure you consider the possible **consequences** of your solution – positive and negative.

You're weighing up the costs and benefits of the solution for the stakeholders in the case. If part of your solution for the teacher in the aggressive child case is for her to spend some one-on-one time with the child in the classroom, what would be the cost to the other children in the class? Is it justified in terms of the benefits it will bring? Could anything be done to lessen this cost?

A crucial part of presenting any solution is to justify it. We'll look at an example using the Moon Dust case.

In justifying your solution you need to provide a rationale (set of reasons) for every part of the solution, supported by the literature and references to the case:

- Why is each step necessary?
- How will it address the issues in the case?
- Is there any order in which the steps should be taken? Why?

Due to the complexity of the problems at Moon Dust Designs, a multi-component intervention will be required to restore productive working relationships and practices in the company.

Reopen channels of communication
Given the currently dysfunctional relationship between the owner and the machinists, it is possible that any proposed changes would be met with suspicion and possibly resistance. So the most immediate requirement will be to restore upward–downward communication between the owner and the machinists in order to start ...

The most urgent step is introduced first, with an explanation of why it's needed and a clear indication of **priority**: 'most immediate requirement'

Notice the student's use of words and phrases to indicate reasons: 'due to'; 'given'; 'so'; 'in order to' repairing this relationship and rebuilding trust in the company. The process can begin with a structured meeting of all staff …

A crucial first step in this process will be for the owner to apologize for the current situation in the company and acknowledge her own mistakes in terms of her lack of experience in managing the changing needs of the company. While apologizing can be extremely difficult, especially in a situation where relationships are dysfunctional, research has shown that comprehensive apologies by leaders can improve trust and repair relationships (Byrne et al. 2013) … Gillespie and Dietz (2009) identify four components of a comprehensive apology. These include: …

The student uses words and phrases to indicate the **sequence** of the steps required in the process: 'begin with'; 'first step' and their **importance**: `crucial`

Always explain **why** each part of the solution is necessary and **how** it can be done, with reference to the case and the literature.

Notice how specific the student's advice is – not only justifying the use of apology but also explaining exactly how this should be done to be effective. What the student is really providing here is a form of *action plan* for the client – **what** should be done, **when** and **how**, and **who** should be involved.

18 Developing an action plan

Many case study assignments require you to develop a detailed action plan for the implementation of your recommended solution. For each objective, there needs to be a clear plan of the steps involved; otherwise the solution is likely to fail.

What will need to be done?
Does your solution involve a series of interrelated steps? Do some of the steps need to be completed before others can begin?

Who will be involved in doing it?
Think very carefully about who needs to be involved in different parts of your solution. For example, should the machinists in the Moon Dust case be involved in the allocation of people to teams and the choice of team leaders? What does the literature say about this? Make sure all your decisions are informed and supported by the readings.

How will it be done?
Some assignments will require a step-by-step description of the process involved in implementing your solution. If this is a technical assignment, you might need to provide drawings or photographs illustrating the process. It might also be useful to include a flow chart showing the process or series of steps involved. Don't forget to label any visual materials appropriately (e.g. Figure 3 Mounting the scaffolding). Also refer the reader to figures in any explanation (e.g. see Figure 3).

 ANALYZING A CASE STUDY

What resources will be required?

Check your assignment briefs carefully for details about this – some assignments might require calculations of costs involved. If you're providing these, make sure you include the formula you used for the calculation when you write up your assignment.

When will it be done?

Solutions often require timelines – how long should each step take? Some assignments will require you to provide dates of completion. Make sure these are realistic given the constraints in the context. If you're shipping in parts from another country, do the research to find out how long this is likely to take. Don't leave this part of the assignment to the last minute – your details must be accurate and realistic.

How will the effectiveness of the solution be monitored/measured?

It's absolutely crucial to monitor the success of solutions so that if anything starts going wrong, there's some kind of early warning system in place to allow for timely interventions and changes or adjustments to be made. Are there specific tools available for monitoring the effectiveness of your solution? What does the literature say about this? At what point should the success of the solution start to be monitored?

And with that we've come full circle with our problem-solving loop! On the next page I've drawn a modified version of the loop by adding some of the advice covered in the book.

Your analysis is informed by the context of the case and the literature all the way through:

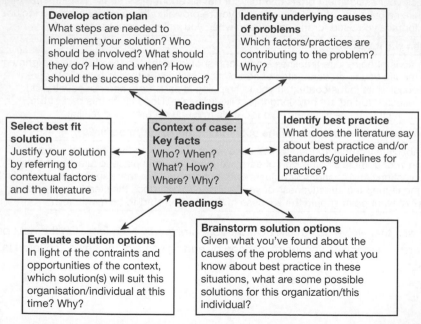

Develop action plan
What steps are needed to implement your solution? Who should be involved? What should they do? How and when? How should the success be monitored?

Identify underlying causes of problems
Which factors/practices are contributing to the problem? Why?

Readings

Select best fit solution
Justify your solution by referring to contextual factors and the literature

Context of case: Key facts
Who? When? What? How? Where? Why?

Identify best practice
What does the literature say about best practice and/or standards/guidelines for practice?

Readings

Evaluate solution options
In light of the contraints and opportunities of the context, which solution(s) will suit this organisation/individual at this time? Why?

Brainstorm solution options
Given what you've found about the causes of the problems and what you know about best practice in these situations, what are some possible solutions for this organization/this individual?

References

Ellet W (2007) *The Case Study Handbook: How to Read, Discuss and Write Persuasively About Cases*. Boston: Harvard Business School Press.

Eunson B (2008) *Communicating in the 21st Century*. (2nd edn). Milton: Wiley.

Hannagan T (2008) *Management Concepts and Practices* (5th edn). Harlow: Pearson.

Huber G P (1980) *Managerial Decision Making*. Glenview: Scott, Foresman and Company.

Useful Sources

Godfrey J (2014) *Reading and Making Notes*. Basingstoke: Palgrave Macmillan.

Godwin J (2014) *Planning Your Essay* (2nd edn). Basingstoke: Palgrave Macmillan.

Hartley P and Dawson M (2010) *Success in Groupwork*. Basingstoke: Palgrave Macmillan.

Reid M (2012) *Report Writing*. Basingstoke: Palgrave Macmillan.

University of Manchester (2015) *Academic Phrasebank*. Available at www.click2go. umip.com/i/academic_phrasebank/appe.html.

Williams K (2014) *Getting Critical* (2nd edn). Basingstoke: Palgrave Macmillan.

Index